MAR - - 2013

21st
Century
Skills Library

COOL MILITARY CAREERS

SPECIAL OPS

JOSH GREGORY

CHERRY
LAKE
Publishing

Published in the United States of America by
Cherry Lake Publishing, Ann Arbor, Michigan
www.cherrylakepublishing.com

Content Adviser
Cynthia Watson, PhD, author of *U.S. National Security*

Credits
Cover and page 1, ©Michael Wood/Dreamstime.com; pages 6, 9, and 20,
©ASSOCIATED PRESS; page 6, U.S. Navy photo by Mass Communication Specialist
3rd Class Blake Midnight/Released; page 10, U.S. Army photo by Spc. Daniel P. Shook/
Released; page 12, U.S. Air Force photo by Senior Airman Jason Epley/Released;
page 15, U.S. Marine Corps photo by Lance Cpl. Kyle McNally/Released; page 16,
U.S. Air Force photo by Tech. Sgt. DeNoris A. Mickle/Released; page 18, U.S. Navy
photo by Mass Communication Specialist 2nd Class Shauntae Hinkle-Lymas/Released;
page 23, DoD photo by Mass Communication Specialist 2nd Class Kyle D. Gahlau,
U.S. Navy/Released; page 25, DoD photo by Mass Communication Specialist 3rd Class
Blake Midnight, U.S. Navy/Released; page 26, U.S. Army photo by Spc. Justin A. Naylor/
Released; page 28, ©Alex Segre/Alamy

Library of Congress Cataloging-in-Publication Data
Gregory, Josh.
  Special ops/by Josh Gregory.
      p. cm.—(Cool military careers) (21st century skills library)
  Includes bibliographical references and index.
  Audience: Grades 4–6.
  ISBN 978-1-61080-446-2 (lib. bdg.) — ISBN 978-1-61080-533-9 (e-book) —
ISBN 978-1-61080-620-6 (pbk.)
  1. Special forces (Military science)—United States—Juvenile literature.
  2. United States—Armed Forces—Vocational guidance—Juvenile literature.
  I. Title. II. Title: Special operations.
  UA34.S64G745 2011
  356'.160973—dc23   2012001721

Cherry Lake Publishing would like to acknowledge
the work of The Partnership for 21st Century Skills.
Please visit *www.21stcenturyskills.org* for more information.

Printed in the United States of America
Corporate Graphics Inc.
July 2012
CLFA11

COOL MILITARY CAREERS

TABLE OF CONTENTS

CHAPTER ONE
A JOB UNLIKE ANY OTHER

Late at night on May 2, 2011, two U.S. helicopters flew toward a walled-in mansion in Abbottabad, Pakistan. The first helicopter dropped off 11 members of the U.S. Navy's

Osama bin Laden was one of the world's most wanted terrorist leaders.

Sea, Air, and Land Teams (SEALs), a translator, and a dog just outside the compound. Wearing night-vision goggles, seven of the SEALs used explosives to blast through the metal gates. The other four SEALs, the translator, and the dog worked to prevent **civilians** from the surrounding neighborhood from approaching the area.

Meanwhile, the second helicopter flew over the top of the compound's 12-foot (3.7-meter) walls, which were topped with barbed wire. Twelve more SEALs slid down ropes from the helicopter to the compound. They began working their way into the compound's buildings and soon met up with the seven SEALs who had blasted through the gates. Together, they fought through the compound until they met their target.

Several months earlier, the U.S. military had learned that terrorist leader Osama bin Laden was hiding out in the Abbottabad compound. Bin Laden was responsible for planning the terrorist attacks of September 11, 2001, and the U.S. military had been hunting him ever since. The SEALs' raid on his compound was the result of several months of hard work and planning. All the hard work paid off. After making their way into the compound, the SEALs killed bin Laden. All 23 SEALs, the translator, and the dog boarded helicopters and made their escape.

■ ■ ■

The Navy SEALs are just one of the U.S. military's special operations forces. These special forces are tasked with the military's most important and dangerous missions, such as the raid on Osama bin Laden's compound. Special forces are ready to travel anywhere at any time. They are made up of the military's most highly trained soldiers. Many are experts

Navy SEALs are among the most highly trained fighters in the military.

in swimming, parachuting, and diving. Almost all of them are trained to use the world's most advanced weapons. They can survive anywhere in the world for as long as they need in almost any conditions.

Special forces are called in to complete missions that other members of the military are not trained to handle. They often travel deep into enemy territory and operate under extreme secrecy. Many special operations missions take place in areas where the government must be careful not to anger foreign leaders. Military leaders can trust the members of the special forces to complete missions quickly and correctly.

Some special operations missions are direct actions. These missions often involve the destruction of important enemy targets. Such targets could be weapons, communications systems, or even important enemy leaders. Other direct actions include clearing out minefields or using **sabotage** to disable enemy resources.

Special forces are also called in regularly to complete **reconnaissance** missions. The soldiers sneak into enemy territory to observe troop movements and figure out what enemies are planning to do next. They often enter these dangerous areas by parachuting or swimming. They avoid being seen and relay important information back to their own leaders.

Special forces are sometimes responsible for organizing and training potential allies in enemy territory. These allies are often rebel groups that want to defeat their countries' governments with the help of the United States. Special forces teach the groups military tactics, show them how to use weapons, and help them plan attacks.

In the years since the terrorist attacks of September 11, 2001, special forces have become a major part of the war against terrorism. They use all of their abilities to hunt down and eliminate terrorists in dangerous foreign nations. They investigate potential terrorist attacks and work to prevent such attacks from succeeding. Special forces also help prevent terrorism by training foreign militaries or rebel groups to help fight terrorists.

Have you ever thought about doing these sorts of jobs? Becoming a member of the U.S. military's special forces can be an exciting and rewarding challenge. Members of the special forces know that each and every one of their missions has an important effect on the world. However, being in the special forces is not just about adventure and excitement. It is also incredibly difficult and dangerous. These amazing people risk their lives every day to help protect the United States and preserve peace throughout the world.

The terrorist attacks of September 11, 2001, were the most devastating in U.S. history.

CHAPTER TWO
READY FOR ANYTHING

Members of the special forces can never be certain what the next day will bring. They travel all around the world, completing a wide variety of missions.

Members of the special forces must learn how to operate advanced weaponry.

A member of the special forces might find himself driving a snow machine across enemy lines one day and calling in an air strike the next.

Like the rest of the military, members of the special forces are divided into two basic categories. Officers fill leadership positions. They command groups of soldiers, plan missions, and train less-experienced members. Enlisted personnel make up the rest of the special forces. The U.S. Army, Air Force, Navy, and Marine Corps have their own special forces. Each branch has its own specialties, and there are many different responsibilities within each one.

The Army makes up the largest part of the United States' special forces. Its roughly 26,000 special forces members are spread across two categories. The first is known simply as the Army Special Forces. Its members are often called Green Berets, after the hats that are part of their uniforms. The Green Berets are divided into six specialties that work together in teams to accomplish their goals.

Each team is usually made up of 12 members. An officer leads the group. He is responsible for leading the team through its mission, from explaining mission **objectives** to gathering necessary equipment. He must be able to think quickly and make difficult decisions while under incredible pressure.

Engineer sergeants assist the team with a variety of technical tasks. They are responsible for carrying out sabotage missions or using explosives to destroy enemy structures. They also design and oversee the construction of bridges, **fortifications**, and other structures that might be needed to accomplish a mission. Their knowledge also makes them helpful in reading maps of enemy territory and determining the best ways to cross difficult **terrain**.

Army Rangers sometimes parachute deep into enemy territory.

Medical sergeants are an important part of any Green Beret team. Serious injuries are a constant risk for members of the special forces. Medical sergeants provide emergency care to Green Berets who are wounded in the field. They also give potential allies medical screenings. This is to make sure the allies are healthy enough to fight and do not have contagious diseases that could spread to U.S. forces.

Communications sergeants are in charge of installing, operating, and maintaining communications equipment in the field. This allows the Green Berets to relay important information back to their superiors. It also enables them to receive new orders if a situation changes.

Weapons sergeants are in charge of combat operations. While all members of the Green Berets are highly trained in the use of weapons, it is the weapons sergeants who decide which targets to attack. They complete tasks such as clearing minefields and using explosives to take out enemy targets. Weapons sergeants also train and equip allies encountered behind enemy lines.

The Army's second special operations group is the 75th Ranger Regiment. Rangers are the most elite soldiers in the Army. They focus mainly on combat missions. Military leaders use Army Rangers when they need important reconnaissance or quick, powerful attacks on enemies. Rangers are also sent into enemy territory to rescue prisoners of war or capture enemy leaders. Many of their missions are based on getting into and out of enemy territory as quickly as possible.

The Navy SEALs are another of the military's elite special forces. They are trained to fight and survive at sea, in the air, and on land. They are called in to complete missions similar to those of the Army Rangers. They use advanced tactics and the latest technology to engage in direct action, gather **intelligence**, and capture enemies.

21ST CENTURY CONTENT

The Marine Corps Special Operations Command (MARSOC) is the newest part of the U.S. military's special forces. It was officially established in 2005. Like other special forces, MARSOC Marines complete a variety of combat, reconnaissance, and demolition missions in the most dangerous parts of the world. MARSOC is the smallest of the country's special forces, but it continues to grow. If you are interested in a special forces career, you might want to consider this new organization.

MARSOC Marines are among the newest additions to the U.S. special forces.

The SEALs are not the only special forces in the Navy. Aviation Rescue Swimmers dive deep into ocean waters to rescue people from aircraft crashes. Explosive ordnance disposal technicians locate and identify explosive devices planted by enemies. Then they work to either disable the devices or detonate them safely. They often work with other special forces teams, such as SEALs or Green Berets, when their expertise

Members of the Air Force special forces conduct many of their operations from the sky.

is needed. Navy divers salvage equipment and information from sunken ships or other underwater wreckage. They also assist in construction or demolition projects that take place underwater. Special warfare combatant-craft crewmen operate boats in rivers, lakes, and other small bodies of water. They often work to insert other special forces into dangerous areas and then get them out when the job is done.

The U.S. Air Force's special tactics teams work mainly to coordinate the use of aircraft in enemy territory. There are three main jobs within the organization. Combat controllers plan and manage air traffic. Like civilian air traffic controllers, they must be certified by the Federal Aviation Administration (FAA). Combat controllers ensure the safety of U.S. aircraft by keeping track of flight plans and alerting pilots of dangers on the ground. Special operations weather team specialists provide important weather information to pilots. They use a variety of high-tech equipment to monitor the weather in combat zones and make forecasts to help pilots and controllers plan safe and effective flight missions. Pararescue specialists parachute into dangerous areas to rescue injured or stranded soldiers. They are also trained in emergency medical procedures and survival methods.

Between them, these special forces are able to tackle almost any problem. However, members of the special forces do not become experts in their jobs overnight. It takes an incredible amount of hard work and natural ability to succeed in special operations.

CHAPTER THREE
TOUGH TRAINING

Special operations jobs are among the most difficult the military has to offer. As a result, potential members of the special forces face the military's most difficult

Members of the special forces must be in excellent physical shape.

training programs. Before pursuing a special forces career, be sure that it is a good fit for you.

All members of the special forces must be extremely strong and athletic. They are often required to carry heavy loads on foot for long distances. Training programs require them to run long distances at high speeds. They also need to be very strong to operate certain weapons properly. Because women are typically not large or strong enough to complete many of these tasks, they are not currently allowed to join special forces.

Quick thinking and decision-making abilities are also important in the special forces. Members of the special forces can never predict what they will encounter on a mission. They must always be ready to react and adapt to new developments. They must also be good leaders and able to follow orders. Teamwork is a necessary part of all military jobs. Being able to put aside personal differences and get a job done can be the difference between life and death.

If you are thinking of a career in the military, be sure to study math, science, and technology in school. These subjects will be helpful in almost any military career. Participate in team sports to develop your athletic abilities and teamwork.

Once you have decided on a special forces career, there are several paths you can take to reach your goal. The most common way is to enlist after graduating from high school.

The enlistment process begins by visiting a **recruiter**. Recruiters can answer any questions you have about the military. They can help you figure out if you are a good candidate for the special forces.

You can also enter the military by getting a college degree and becoming an officer. One way of doing this is to attend one of the U.S. military's colleges, such as the U.S. Naval Academy in Annapolis, Maryland; the U.S. Military Academy

ROTC members train for military service while attending college.

in West Point, New York; or the U.S. Air Force Academy in Colorado Springs, Colorado. These schools are very competitive, but all graduates become officers in the military in addition to receiving college degrees. Another way to become an officer is to join the Reserve Officers' Training Corps (ROTC) program at a civilian school. Members of these programs participate in drills and training exercises while working on their degrees. They become officers upon graduation. Finally, college graduates without any military experience can become officers by attending officer candidate school in the branch of their choice.

LEARNING & INNOVATION SKILLS

Even if you are an excellent student and an amazing athlete, military training will not be easy. It involves intense physical and mental stress that most civilians never experience. For example, only about half of the candidates who begin Army Ranger School are able to finish the program and graduate. About 60 percent of those who fail do so in the first four days of the two-month program. If you truly want to succeed in the special forces, you can never give up.

Not all members of the military are eligible to join the special forces. Candidates for the special forces must also pass a variety of tests to qualify. Like all enlisted members of the military, they begin by taking a test called the Armed Services Vocational Aptitude Battery (ASVAB). The ASVAB tests new recruits on a variety of topics, including math and technical abilities. You will need a very high score on the ASVAB if you want to join special forces. You will also need to pass a variety of intelligence and physical fitness tests. Test content varies slightly depending on the exact job you hope to do. Finally, you will need to be a U.S. citizen.

All newly enlisted members of the military begin their careers with basic training. This program lasts several weeks and involves a variety of drills and exercises designed to prepare new recruits for basic military duties. After basic training, candidates for special forces begin the long process of advanced training.

Qualifying and training for the special forces can take well over a year. Most training programs are made up of several stages. For example, Navy SEALs begin with Basic Underwater Demolition/SEAL (BUD/S) training. This seven-month program is broken into three phases. The first consists mainly of physical conditioning to prepare SEAL candidates for the rest of the program. The second phase teaches a variety of diving techniques. The third focuses on

BUD/S training gives SEALs the skills they need to succeed on dangerous missions.

land combat training. After BUD/S, SEALs begin parachute training. After that, they finally move on to the 26-week SEAL Qualification Training. This program teaches them the advanced sea, air, and land tactics they will use in the field.

Many members of the special forces also go through additional training in specialized skills. They might learn to speak foreign languages or perform medical procedures. Others train to become **snipers** or use more advanced weapons. Training never ends for members of special forces. They must stay up-to-date with the latest technology at all times. They also spend time completing **simulations** to practice their tactics. All of this training adds up to an incredible amount of work, but it all pays off when it comes time to complete a difficult mission.

Two special forces members train
to use explosive devices.

CHAPTER FOUR
THE FUTURE OF SPECIAL OPERATIONS

A s with most military jobs, demand for special forces members changes depending on several factors. More are needed during times of war than during peacetime. It also

Future events will determine how many new special forces members will be needed in the years to come.

depends on how many people are hoping to join the special forces at any given time. For example, the U.S. civilian job market had been struggling for several years leading up to 2011. As a result, many more people than usual were joining the military.

Military salaries do not change from job to job or between the different branches. Instead, they are based on **rank** and experience. In 2011, enlisted personnel earned between about $18,000 and $86,000. Officers have higher salaries. They made between $45,000 and $227,230 that year. The military generally increases all salaries slightly each year to keep up with **inflation**.

Base salaries are not the only source of income for members of the military. They can also earn a variety of bonuses. Some of the bonuses are paid to people with special skills such as being able to speak a foreign language or operate a certain type of equipment. Other bonuses are paid out to new recruits or for special achievements. For example, a bonus of $15,000 is awarded to new Navy SEALs.

Members of the military receive free food, clothing, and housing. These things are not typically offered in civilian jobs. Members of the military are also provided with free medical care and excellent retirement benefits. They can retire after just 20 years of service. Most people join the military when they are in their late teens or early twenties. This means they can retire at much younger ages than people in most civilian jobs can.

Early retirement leaves former members of the military free to pursue new careers or further education. The military offers career services to help retirees find new jobs and scholarships to help them pay for education. Many retirees find that the skills they learned in the military carry over to civilian jobs. Former members of the special forces often find work in law enforcement or private security companies.

Some special forces members become police officers after leaving the military.

LIFE & CAREER SKILLS

Being able to use advanced weaponry or parachute out of high-flying aircraft are important skills for members of the special forces. But they are not very useful in most civilian jobs. This doesn't mean that special forces members aren't suited to begin new careers. In fact, their leadership skills and strong work ethic make them excellent candidates for management jobs. Many former members of special forces go on to become managers in civilian businesses.

Former Air Force combat controllers might find jobs as civilian flight controllers. Those with medical experience might seek out additional training and take jobs as physician's assistants. Others return to college and study to begin careers that are entirely different from what they did in the military.

For as long as there are conflicts around the world, the special forces will be an important part of the U.S. military. These amazing men devote incredible amounts of energy to keeping the United States safe from its enemies. Joining their ranks is a long and difficult task, but with enough hard work, you could be one of them. Do you have what it takes?

GLOSSARY

civilians (suh-VIL-yuhnz) people who are not members of the military

fortifications (for-tuh-fuh-KAY-shunz) walls or other structures built for protection

inflation (in-FLAY-shuhn) a general increase in prices

intelligence (in-TEL-uh-juhnts) information gathered and used by government agencies to plan and make important decisions

objectives (uhb-JEK-tivz) goals a person is trying to achieve

rank (RANGK) official job level or position

reconnaissance (ruh-KAHN-uh-suhns) exploration to gain information about enemy forces or unfamiliar territory

recruiter (ri-KROO-tur) a military employee in charge of signing up new members and providing information to people who are interested in joining the military

sabotage (SAB-uh-tahzh) deliberate damage or destruction of property, especially to prevent or stop an event or action

simulations (sim-yuh-LAY-shuhnz) trial runs to act out real events

snipers (SNIPE-urz) soldiers who are trained to fire guns accurately from faraway or hidden locations

terrain (tuh-RAYN) the surface features of an area of land

FOR MORE INFORMATION

BOOKS

Adams, Simon. *Eyewitness Soldier*. New York: DK Publishing, 2009.

Alvarez, Carlos. *Army Rangers*. Minneapolis, MN: Bellwether Media, 2010.

Gonzalez, Lissette. *The U.S. Military: Defending the Nation*. New York: PowerKids Press, 2008.

Yomtov, Nel. *Navy SEALs in Action*. New York: Bearport Publishing, 2008.

WEB SITES

Navy SEALs
www.sealswcc.com/seal-default.aspx
Visit the official Web site of the U.S. Navy SEALs to learn about the group's history, training programs, and missions.

U.S. Army—75th Ranger Regiment
www.goarmy.com/ranger.html
Find out more about what it takes to become an Army Ranger.

INDEX

ABOUT THE AUTHOR

Josh Gregory edits and writes books for kids. He lives in Chicago, Illinois.